Crazy about Cats

DIANE WARD

illustrated
by Martin Maass

Struik Publishers
(A division of New Holland Publishing
(South Africa) (Pty) Ltd)
Cornelis Struik House
80 McKenzie Street
Cape Town
8001

New Holland Publishing is a member of the
Johnnic Publishing Group.

www.struik.co.za

Log on to our photographic website
www.imagesofafrica.co.za
for an African experience.

First published in 2005

10 9 8 7 6 5 4 3 2 1

Publishing manager: Pippa Parker
Managing editor: Lynda Ingham-Brown
Designer: Janice Evans
Cover design: Janice Evans
Proofreader: Cecilia Barfield

Reproduction by Hirt and Carter Cape (Pty) Ltd
Printed and bound by Times Offset, Malaysia

ISBN 1 77007 268 3

DEDICATED TO
Tamarin, Jennifer, David and Matthew and the light
you bring to the world.

And to Garfield for his years of love and patience
in making us all well-trained humans.

THANKS TO
Dr John Down Veterinarian
The Thorn Brook Veterinary Clinic, High Peak
Sarah Maritz, Faculty of Veterinary Science,
Onderstepoort
Hanne Gent, Reform Haus

Contents

Introduction 4
Curious Cat Facts 6

Beds for relaxation 8
Pillow bed 9
Tepee bed 12
Basket bed 16
Travelling bed 18

Food for Thought 22
Tom Quartz Cookies 24
Solomon's Treats 25
Muessa's Ribbon Biscuits 26
Micestto's Medley 29
Williamina's Sardines
and Rice 30
Garfield's Gourmet
Supper 33
Margate's Mackerel
Munchies 34
Cheshire's Choice 35

Toys for Fun 36
Simple sisal toy 38
Catnip 40
Catnip mouse 41
Catnip treat ball 44
Feather wands 47
Raffia pompoms 48
Hanging toys 50
Scratching post 53
Quickies 55

Gift ideas 56
Jingly Collar 57
Placemats 58
Festive Gift Sack 60
Potato Prints 62
Feline Frames 64
Purrfect Pawprints 67

**Caring for Orphaned
Kittens 68**
Warmth and first aid 70
Feeding an
orphaned kitten 71
Weaning 74
Toilet training 74
Fleas and parasites 75
Milestones 75

Grooming 76
Tools required 78

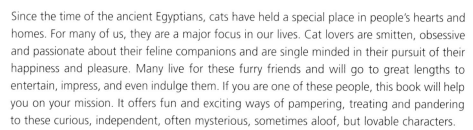

Introduction

Since the time of the ancient Egyptians, cats have held a special place in people's hearts and homes. For many of us, they are a major focus in our lives. Cat lovers are smitten, obsessive and passionate about their feline companions and are single minded in their pursuit of their happiness and pleasure. Many live for these furry friends and will go to great lengths to entertain, impress, and even indulge them. If you are one of these people, this book will help you on your mission. It offers fun and exciting ways of pampering, treating and pandering to these curious, independent, often mysterious, sometimes aloof, but lovable characters.

Cats are amazing creatures. They can accomplish great feats and are extremely agile; they can leap from a standing start five times their own height with seemingly little effort, climb impossible obstacles, and balance along the top of very narrow walkways. They have nimble feet that are so sensitive they can feel the vibrations of their prey moving in the dark. Cats can see in light six times dimmer than humans can, and have whiskers so sensitive they can feel the air move around a solid object in the dark. The cat can move its ears independently through 180 degrees and hear up to 60 kHz. Its sense of smell and taste are so heightened it can pick up a huge amount of information from its surroundings, not only the present situation but also the recent past. They can identify individual cats that have passed through the area up to a week previously.

This book will help educate cat-lovers about the needs of our cats and will enable them to enjoy their pets to the fullest. The toys, beds and recipes in this book are designed to be cost effective, quick and easy to make. They are as much fun for adults as they are for children. In encouraging our children to care for their pet's every need we are guiding them to becoming caring, mature adults who will value all animal life and their environment.

Curious cat facts

★ A cat's sense of smell is 30 times more acute than humans' sense of smell.

★ Relative to its body size, the cat has a larger brain than all mammals except for primates and dolphins.

★ A male ginger tabby cat in Canada is on record for having 28 toes, seven on each paw.

★ The most searched for animal on the Internet is the domestic cat.

★ The world's smallest cat, Tinker Toy, is just 7 cm tall at the shoulder and 19 cm long (about the size of a cheque book).

★ Kittens are born with their eyes closed; when they first open them they are always blue.

★ Cats usually have litters of between one and ten kittens; the largest litter on record was 19 Persian/Burmese cross kittens born in the UK in 1970.

★ Cats have baby teeth that start to fall out at about 4 months.

* The Manx is a breed of cat that has no tail.
* Humans have 18 times more taste buds than cats.
* The ancient Egyptians worshipped the cat goddess Bastet.
* The oldest feline mother gave birth to two kittens at the ripe old age of 30.
* The heaviest cat recorded weighed in at a staggering 21,3kg.

* The oldest cat on record lived to be 36 years old.
* Cats have five toes on each front paw, but only four toes on each back paw.
* The most kittens produced by a domestic cat is recorded to be 420 kittens in her lifetime.
* The first ever official cat show was held in London in 1871. They have since become popular worldwide.

Beds for

Relaxation

Pillow Bed

Cats are the world's best sleepers, slumbering away 70% of their lives. A typical day for a cat consists of over 15 hours of sleeping and dozing time.

You will need

1,5 m fabric (115 cm wide) for inner pillow
1,6 m fabric (115 cm wide) for outer cover
Cotton for sewing
Three press studs
1 bag stuffing
Pins

To make the inner pillow (see overleaf)

- Cut two pieces of fabric measuring 14 cm x 75 cm (2 x A).
- Cut two pieces of fabric measuring 14 cm x 50 cm (2 x B).
- With right sides facing, pin the shortest side of one strip A to the shortest side of one strip B and sew together. Repeat this until all four pieces are joined together and you have the rectangle that forms the sides of the pillow.
- Cut two pieces of fabric measuring 50 cm x 75 cm; these will form the top and bottom of the inner pillow.

BEDS FOR RELAXATION

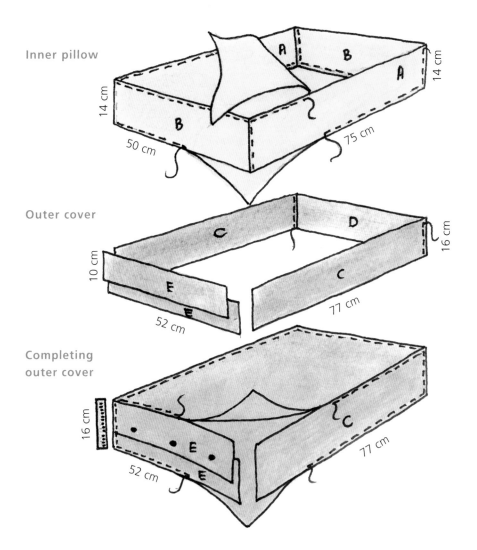

Inner pillow

14 cm

14 cm

A

B

A

B

50 cm

75 cm

Outer cover

16 cm

C

D

10 cm

C

E

E

52 cm

77 cm

Completing
outer cover

16 cm

E

E

C

52 cm

77 cm

- With right sides facing, pin the sides of the pillow to the top and bottom of the pillow. Sew around the edges leaving an opening large enough to turn the pillow right side out.
- Turn the pillow right side out and fill with stuffing. Hand sew the opening closed.

To make the outer cover

- Cut two pieces of fabric measuring 16 cm x 77 cm (2 x C).
- Cut one piece of fabric measuring 16 cm x 52 cm (1 x D).
- Position strip D between the two C strips, shortest ends together, right sides facing, pin and sew together along the shortest edges.
- Cut two pieces of fabric measuring 10 cm x 52 cm (2 x E). This will form the opening envelope.
- Hem along one of long edges of each piece E. Place the two pieces on top of each other, overlapping them so they measure 16 cm as shown in the diagram. Pin and sew them to the shortest edges of each strip C and complete the rectangle that will form the sides of the outer cover.
- Cut two pieces of fabric measuring 77 cm x 52 cm for the top and bottom of the pillow cover. With right sides facing, pin the top and bottom to the side panels and sew together.
- Turn the pillow cover right side out and sew the press-studs into place at the opening envelope. Insert the inner pillow.

Tepee Bed

Some cats like sleeping in confined, dark spaces and the tepee bed is perfect for this.

You will need

Triangular cardboard template
  50 cm x 50 cm x 50 cm
Triangular cardboard
  template 20 cm x 20 cm x 20 cm
2 m fabric (115 cm wide)
5 m bias binding
1/2 m quilting foam/batting
Thread and pins

To make the tepee

- Using the larger triangular template, cut out eight triangles of fabric and four triangles of foam (see diagram 1).
- Take two triangles of fabric, place them right sides facing, and place a piece of foam on top of this, pin together and sew around two sides.
- Turn right side out and sew closed the bottom edge.
- Make another three triangles in the same way so that you have four sides.

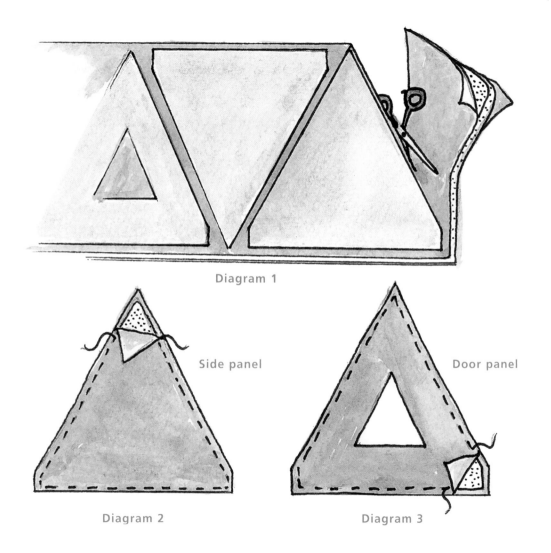

Diagram 1

Side panel

Diagram 2

Door panel

Diagram 3

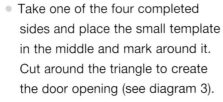

To make the door panel

- Take one of the four completed sides and place the small template in the middle and mark around it. Cut around the triangle to create the door opening (see diagram 3).

- Fold in the edges of the opening and hem, or neaten the edges by encasing them with bias binding.

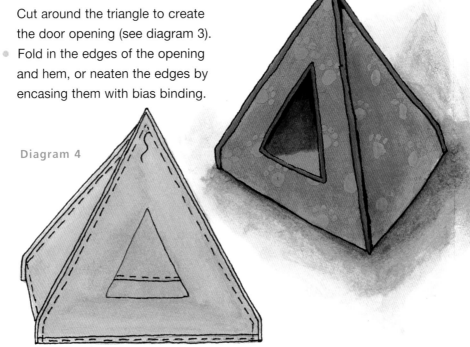

Completed bed

Diagram 4

To make the base

- Cut two pieces of fabric measuring 50 cm x 50 cm.
- Cut one piece of foam measuring 50 cm x 50 cm.
- With right sides facing, pin together the two pieces of fabric and place the foam on top. Sew all the way around the square leaving an opening large enough to turn right side out.
- Turn right side out and sew the opening closed.

To make up

- Align each triangular side to a corresponding side of the base and pin in place. Stitch the side panels to the base.

- Turn so seams are on the inside of the bed and pin the sides together to form the triangular shape of the tepee (see diagram 4).
- Sew the sides of the triangles together on the outside and use the bias binding to encase the seams.

Basket Bed

When 'catnapping', cats close their eyes but remain alert. If they are going to settle into a deep sleep they need to find a place where they feel safe and secure.

You will need
1 m fabric (115 cm wide)
1/2 m quilting foam/batting
Circular cardboard template, diameter 40 cm
Pins and thread

To make
- Cut two pieces of fabric measuring 62 cm x 18 cm for the side panel of the bed.
- Cut one piece of foam measuring 62 cm x 18 cm.
- Place the side panels of fabric together with right sides facing, put the foam on top, pin together and sew around three sides leaving one of the short sides open.
- Turn right side out and sew the open edge closed. Pin and sew the two shortest sides together to form a circle, this will be the side panel of the bed.
- Using the circlular template, cut two circles of fabric and one circle of foam.
- Take the two fabric circles and place them right sides facing, put the foam

circle on top of them, pin together and sew around the edge leaving an opening large enough to turn the base right side out.

- Turn right side out and sew the opening closed.
- Carefully pin the side panel of the bed to the base and sew around the edges to attach the side panel to the base of the bed.

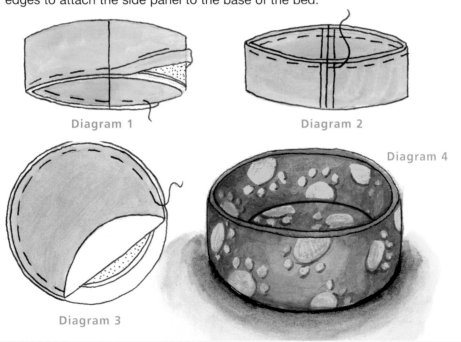

Diagram 1

Diagram 2

Diagram 4

Diagram 3

Travelling Bed

According to the *Guinness Book of Records* the world's most travelled cat was one called Hamlet. He escaped from his carrier while on a flight from Toronto, Canada, and was found seven weeks later behind a panel in the plane. He had travelled approximately 600 000 km.

You will need

1,5 m fabric
1,5 m quilting
   foam/batting
5,5 m bias binding
8 pieces ribbon
   18 cm long
Pins and thread

To make the sides of the bed

- Cut four pieces of fabric measuring 40 cm x 20 cm.
- Cut two pieces of foam measuring 40 cm x 20 cm.
- Take two pieces of fabric, place right sides facing, and put a piece of foam on top. Pin together and sew around three edges, leaving one of the longest sides open, this is the base (bottom) edge. Turn right side out.

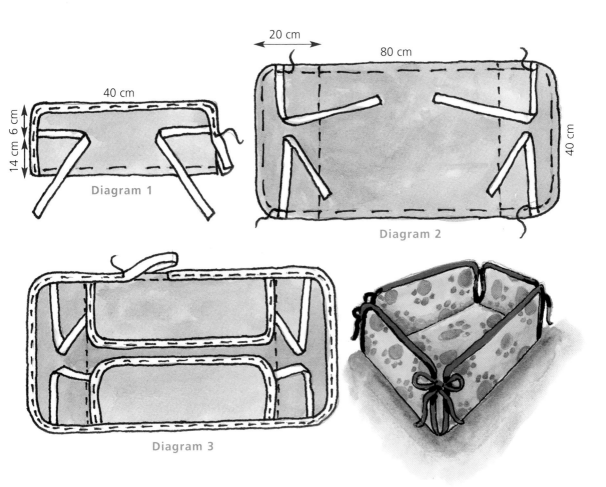

40 cm

14 cm 6 cm

Diagram 1

20 cm

80 cm

40 cm

Diagram 2

Diagram 3

Diagram 4

When choosing a spot for
your cat's new bed, look
for a place that offers
both warmth and safety.

- Attach a piece of ribbon to each short side, 6 cm down from the top (sewn) edge as shown in diagram 1.
- Encase the three sewn sides with bias binding, leaving the base edge open.
- Make the second side in the same way.

To make the base

- Cut two pieces of fabric measuring 80 cm x 40 cm.
- Cut one piece of foam measuring 80 cm x 40 cm. Place fabric right sides facing, put the foam on the top, sew around the edges leaving an opening big enough to turn right side out.
- Turn right side out and sew the opening closed.
- Place a piece of ribbon 6 cm in from each corner of the longest sides and sew into place as shown in diagram 2 on page 19.

To make up

- To create the other two sides, sew in a straight line across the width of the base, 20 cm in from the corners (see diagram 2).
- Attach the completed sides between these rows of stitching on each side (see diagram 3).
- Neaten the edges with an overlocker or encase with bias binding.
- Fold up sides and tie into place (see diagram 4).

Food for Thought

Cats require particularly careful feeding because of their rather unusual metabolism. They are obligate carnivores – this means that they require some dietary essentials that can only be found in animal tissues. In the wild their full dietary needs are met by consuming all or most of their prey. Cats cannot live on a vegetarian diet. Feline nutrition is a well-studied science and pet food manufacturers are leaders in the field. Commercially available cat foods have been extensively researched to ensure they meet your cat's complex dietary needs and contribute to short- and long-term health. Using reputable brands of cat food is therefore the quickest and easiest way of feeding your cat.

The recipes in this book are not intended as substitutes for properly balanced, commercially produced products. Although they are nutritious, they alone will not provide the balanced diet your cat needs in order to remain at optimum health. They are designed to serve as occasional treats and to give variety to your cat's diet. Most cats have a low tolerance for lactose, so whenever possible use lactose-free milk in the recipes. A lactose-free product called 'Milk for Cats' is available in good pet shops, or from your local vet.

Tom Quartz Cookies

Tom Quartz was the 'first' feline of the Theodore Roosevelt administration.

You will need

1 cup wholewheat flour
1 teaspoon catnip (available at pet shops)
2 tablespoons wheat germ
1/3 cup powdered milk
1/4 cup soy flour
1 tablespoon molasses
1 egg
2 tablespoons butter or vegetable oil
1/3 cup milk

Preparation

- Preheat oven to 180 °C.
- Mix dry ingredients together.
- Add molasses, egg, oil and milk, and mix together to form a dough.
- Roll out flat, cut into cat bite-sized pieces and place on a greased baking tray.
- Bake for 20 minutes and allow to cool. Store in an airtight container.

Solomon's Treats

Solomon was the long-haired chinchilla who starred in the Bond film *Diamonds are Forever*.

You will need

1 jar (70 grams) strained
   lamb, beef or
   chicken baby food
2/3 cup wheat germ
2/3 cup low-fat powdered milk
1 egg, beaten

Preparation

- Preheat oven to 175 °C.
- Mix all the ingredients together in a bowl.
- Drop 1/2 teaspoonfuls onto a greased baking tray.
- Bake for 12 to 15 minutes.
- Remove from oven and cool.
- Store the treats in an airtight container and refrigerate.

Muessa's Ribbon Biscuits

This cat was so loved by the prophet Mohammed that, according to legend, Mohammed cut off a piece of his robe rather than disturb the cat that was sleeping on it.

You will need

1 cup wholewheat flour

2 tablespoons oil or fat

2 tablespoons wheat germ

1 tablespoon kelp or 1 teaspoon salt
   (kelp comes in powder form and is
   available from most health shops)

1/4 cup soy flour

1/2 teaspoon bone meal

1 tablespoon molasses

1/3 cup milk

Preparation

- Preheat the oven to 175 °C
- Mix all the ingredients together.
- Knead into a dough, roll out and cut into narrow strips or ribbons.
- Place onto a greased baking tray and bake for 25 to 30 minutes until lightly toasted.
- If the biscuits are not hard enough, leave them in the oven with the heat turned off for another 30 minutes. Remove from the oven and allow to cool. Store in an airtight container.

Micestto's Medley

Micestto was born in the Vatican and raised by Pope Leo XII.

You will need

1 cup chicken, boiled (reserve the broth)
1/4 cup fresh broccoli
1/4 cup shredded, steamed carrots

Preparation

- Mix all ingredients together with enough chicken broth to hold the ingredients firm.
- Allow to cool to room temperature before offering.
- Store remainder in a sealed container and refrigerate. Always allow food to warm to room temperature before serving.

FOOD FOR THOUGHT

Williamina's Sardines and Rice

William shared *his* life with Charles Dickens and was promptly renamed Williamina when *her* kittens were born.

You will need

1 tablespoon lightly cooked liver (cooking the liver stops the
   spread of parasites and disease)
2 tins sardines in oil
2/3 cup cooked rice
1/4 cup chopped parsley

Preparation

- Chop the cooked liver finely.
- Break the sardines up into bite-sized pieces.
- Combine sardines and liver with rice and parsley.
- Stir well with a wooden spoon and serve at room temperature.
- Store unused portion in refrigerator, tightly covered.

The ideal temperature for a cat's food is 30 ºC, the same temperature as the cat's tongue.

Garfield's Gourmet Supper

Garfield is the famous three-legged cat who belongs to the Ward family and to whom this book is dedicated. He lost his leg after being hit by a car, but made a remarkable recovery.

You will need

2 tablespoons Bovril/Marmite
1 tablespoon lightly cooked liver
1/3 cup cottage cheese
1 tablespoon olive oil

Preparation

- Dissolve the Bovril/Marmite in a small amount of the juice rendered by cooking the liver.
- Chop the cooked liver finely and add to the Bovril mixture.
- Add the cottage cheese and oil, and mix well.
- Serve at room temperature and store the remaining portion in an airtight container and refrigerate.

Margate's Mackerel Munchies

Margate shared 10 Downing Street with Winston Churchill.

You will need

$1/2$ cup canned mackerel, drained

1 cup cooked white rice

1 tablespoon vegetable oil

1 egg, beaten

$1/2$ teaspoon Brewer's yeast (optional)

Preparation

- Preheat oven to 175 °C.
- In a medium-sized bowl, mash the mackerel well with a fork.
- Combine it with the remaining ingredients and mix well.
- Drop $1/4$ teaspoonfuls of the mixture onto a greased baking tray.
- Bake for 8 minutes.
- Cool to room temperature and store in an airtight container in the refrigerator.

Cheshire's Choice

The Cheshire Cat is described in Lewis Carroll's novel *Alice in Wonderland*. He would disappear leaving only his grin behind.

You will need

1 cup fish, broiled until it flakes (reserve the broth)
1/4 cup cooked rice
1/4 cup mashed, cooked pumpkin or butternut

Preparation

- Mix ingredients with enough fish broth to hold the ingredients together.
- Cool to room temperature before serving.
- Store the remaining portion in an airtight container and refrigerate.

Toys for Fun

Kittens are like young children and learn about the world around them through play. They stalk, chase and pounce on toys in order to develop their hunting skills. These games also provide mental and physical exercise, which is particularly important if they spend a lot of time indoors. Cats need a combination of healthy food and exercise to stay at their healthiest, both mentally and physically. Due to the increased palatability of cat food and the increased number of 'indoor cats', obesity in domestic cats has become a serious problem worldwide. It is essential that indoor cats exercise each day. This can be done by encouraging your cats to play with an assortment of toys. The range of commercially available toys for cats is huge: everything from catnip mice to large activity centres. However, some of the most beloved toys of kittens and cats are homemade, and they are usually inexpensive, simple and fun to make.

Simple Sisal Toy

Sisal toys can be made to look like mice and birds or any other number of objects. They can be attached to wands, pulled along with string or tied to door handles where the cat can reach them easily.

You will need

Any small, used household item that can be covered and will roll such as a small empty bottle, a used cotton reel or rubber ball
A ball of sisal/garden string
A selection of colourful decorations – small feathers, ribbons, beads, bells or fake fur for decoration
Strong, quick-drying glue

To make

- Make sure the base item is clean and contains no chemicals that could harm the cat.
- Wind the string around the item, gluing it down as you go along.
- Attach the decorations to the ends of the item so they create movement when the item is rolled long the ground. Take care to ensure the decorations can't come off the toy and cause choking.

Catnip

Catnip is the common name for a perennial herb of the mint family and, given to the right cat, it can cause an amazing reaction! The cat will rub it, roll over it, kick at it, and generally get very excited for several minutes. The cat might then lose interest and walk away. A few hours later, it may well come back and have exactly the same reaction to the catnip.

As there isn't any scent that causes this sort of reaction in humans, the effects of catnip on cats are difficult for us to understand. However, it is not an uncommon behaviour in animals that rely heavily on their noses.

Although no one knows exactly what happens in the cat's brain, it is known that the chemical nepetalactone in catnip triggers this unique response. It causes a stereotypical response in cats that are sensitive to the chemical. The catnip reaction is inherited, and some cats are totally unaffected by it. Large, wild cats like tigers can be sensitive to it, while very young kittens and much older cats seem less likely to have a reaction to catnip. Cat owners derive great pleasure from the apparent enjoyment by their pets, and catnip is commonly incorporated into cat toys. It may also be applied to the surface of scratching posts to attract a cat's interest. It is available in dried form and marketed as a cat treat. Catnip may be grown in indoor gardens, and is useful for distracting cats from chewing houseplants.

Catnip Mouse

A cat's senses are so refined that by using only its sense of touch and hearing, a blind cat is able to follow a toy along the ground in play and even hunt successfully.

You will need

Tracing paper
Scraps of contrasting material for the body
Felt scraps for the ears
String for the tail
A small bag of dried catnip
Cotton wool for stuffing
Bristles or fishing line for the whiskers
A small bell for the nose
Set of eyes/buttons

To make

- Carefully trace the templates from the next page.
- Cut out the pattern pieces from the fabric and felt.
- With right sides facing, sew the two body pieces together along the back.
- With right sides facing, pin the body to the bottom section of the mouse.

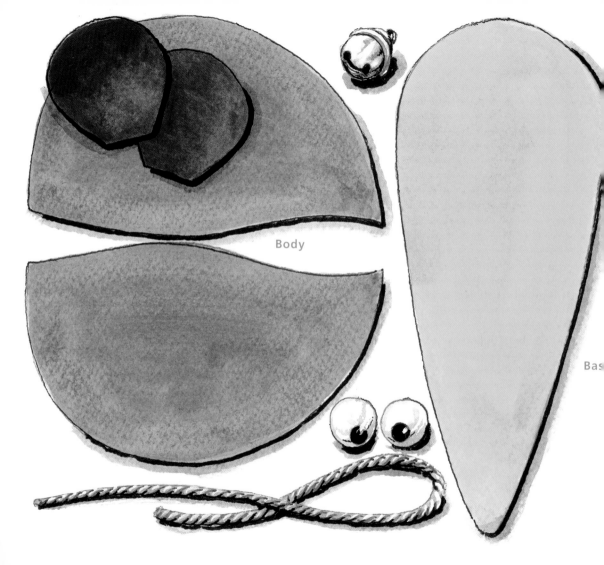

Body

Bas

- Position the tail inside the mouse so the end will be trapped when the seams are sewn.
- Sew around the edges leaving an opening at the nose big enough to turn right side out.
- Turn the mouse right side out and stuff with a mixture of catnip and cotton wool.
- Tie a knot in the middle of each of the whisker bristles and thread each end from the inside out through the fabric in the correct position.
- Sew up the nose of the mouse with the bell and attach the eyes and ears.

Catnip Treat Ball

These treat balls will give your furry friends hours of exercise and entertainment. The ball is filled with catnip treats, which come out as the cat plays with the ball.

You will need
An old tennis ball
A sharp craft knife
Small amount of catnip cat biscuits, available
from most pet shops

To make
- Use a pencil to mark out a hole on the ball. Size is important: if the hole is too small the catnip treats will not come out and if it is too big, they will spill out too quickly. Trace the size of the catnip biscuit onto the tennis ball to get an idea of the size of hole required.
- Hold the tennis ball firmly in your hand and carefully cut around the pencil mark with the craft knife. Make the hole smaller initially if you are unsure; you can always make it bigger later if necessary.
- Fill the ball with the catnip biscuits. If your cat is unsure of his new toy you can rub the outside of the ball with catnip, then sit back and watch the fun.

Feather Wands

Toys that move erratically are often favourites as they arouse a cat's curiosity. Wands are especially useful as they keep your hands far away from kitty's razor-sharp claws.

You will need

An assortment of large beads, feathers and bells
A piece of string or ribbon 50 cm long
A dowel stick around 30 cm long
A glue gun or good quality, strong, quick-drying glue

To make

- Tie the feathers to one end of the string/ribbon.
- Thread the beads and bells onto the string, making sure they can't come off and be swallowed by the cat.
- Attach the string to the end of the dowel stick by tying it on first and then gluing it down.
- This toy will take quite a lot of punishment so make sure the string is well secured. The wands can be as ornate or as simple as you want to make them. Try using recycled items to make your wands as this will keep costs down and encourage creativity.

TOYS FOR FUN

Raffia Pompoms

These raffia pompoms will become a much-loved toy for your cat, not only because they make a wonderful noise when played with, but because their texture is so unusual.

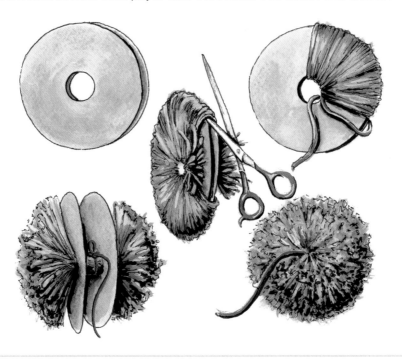

You will need

Compass

A4 piece of medium-thickness cardboard

Raffia strips (or wool)

Darning needle (optional)

Parcel string

To make

- Use the compass to mark out two identical circles from the cardboard (approximately 10 cm in diameter) and cut them out.
- Mark the middle of the circles, and carefully cut out a hole 4 cm in diameter through the middle of both cardboard circles.
- Put the two circles together and start to wind the raffia through the centre of the circles and over the sides. You can thread the raffia onto a darning needle to make it easier to wind it through the centre of the cardboard circles.
- Continue until the sides are completely covered and the centre is closed.
- Carefully cut through the raffia along the outside edges of the two discs.
- Carefully pull the two discs apart and tie the string tightly around the middle of the pompom.
- Once the string has been tied tightly, gently slip the cardboard templates over the raffia and 'fluff' out your pompom.

Hanging Toys

Hanging toys can be useful if your cats are on their own for long periods during the day. They can either be hung on a door handle or in the doorway.

You will need

A length of rope or string
A small beanbag or sisal toy (see page 36)
Large beads or used cotton reels
Feathers, pieces of shiny cloth or ribbons
A screw-in cup hook (if hanging toy from door frame)

To make

- Tie the heaviest item to the bottom end of the string – this gives weight to the toy and will cause it to swing when the cat bats it.
- Tie or thread the chosen beads, feathers and ribbons to the string. Ensure that they are all well secured as cats can be very aggressive in their play.
- Make a loop at the top end of the rope and attach the sisal toy/beanbag to a door handle or suspend it from the cup hook at the top of the doorframe.
- The rope or string should be high enough off the ground so it can swing, but low enough for the cat to reach with a little stretching.

Scratching Post

All cats need to scratch and, contrary to popular belief, do not do so to sharpen their claws, but to remove the outer husk from the sheath of the claw.

You will need

Carpet adhesive and strong wood glue

Carpet off-cuts

Two wooden chipboard squares measuring 30 cm x 30 cm

One wooden post or log measuring approximately 40 cm in length

8 large screws (4 for each platform) and a screwdriver

A ball of thick sisal string or rope

One or more small balls or catnip toys (see p. 42)

Lengths of ribbon to attach the toy/s to the scratching post

To make

- Using the carpet adhesive, glue some of the carpet off-cuts to one of the chipboard squares. Allow the carpet to overlap over the edges of the chipboard square and glue it firmly to the underside.
- Attach the square to the post using four screws to make the base of the

scratching post. Do this from underneath the chipboard square ensuring that the screws go straight into the centre of the post and do not protrude out.

- Cover the post with the wood glue and, starting at one end of the post, wrap the sisal string/rope around it as tightly as possible. Allow the glue to set.
- Attach the second chipboard square to the top of the post using the remaining screws, ensuring that they are flush and do not protrude out of the post where they could hurt the cat. Cover the wooden square with the remaining carpet off-cuts in the same way you did for the base.
- Thread the balls/toys onto lengths of ribbon and glue or nail them to the sides of the top platform so that they hang down.
- Once you have made a simple scratching post, you can design more elaborate scratching posts and activity centres for cats.

Quickies

- A brown paper bag blown up with a puff of air can keep your cat amused for hours.
- A piece of crumpled cellophane that makes crackling and squeaking noises when 'attacked' will be a great success.
- An empty plastic medicine bottle sealed closed with a bean inside it, provides hours of fun.
- A ping-pong ball will always be a favourite toy for cats.
- An empty cardboard box in which the cat can hide and 'ambush' any who dare pass by provides a simple yet effective diversion.

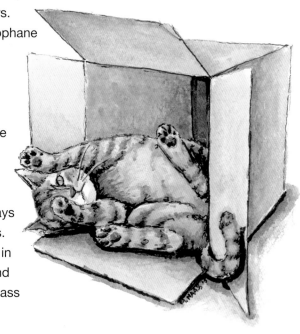

TOYS FOR FUN

Jingly Collar

The Jingly Collar slip goes over a cat's normal collar and can be changed as often as you wish. It allows you to have a selection of fun collars at minimum cost.

You will need

Piece of fabric measuring
   25 cm x 6 cm
Cat collar, with elastic insert
Small bells, jewels
   or beads

To make

- Hem the two short ends of the fabric strip.
- Fold the fabric in half lengthwise with the right sides facing and sew along the long side 1 cm from the edge. Turn right side out.
- Sew on the bells or jewels at equal intervals around the fabric.
- Insert the collar into the slip, allowing the clasp of the collar to protrude.

GIFT IDEAS

Placemats

The templates on the opposite page can be used to make the placemat and the festive gift sack. Template A is used for the placemat, and templates A and B are used for the gift sack.

You will need

Cardboard template (template A opposite can be increased on a
  photocopier by 310 % and used as a pattern)
1 m flexible vinyl
1m iron-on stiffener
1 m bias binding (optional)
Materials to decorate the placemat

To make

- Use template A to cut out two shapes of the vinyl.
- Cut out the same shape from the stiffener.
- Iron the stiffener onto the back of one piece of the vinyl.
- Place the two pieces of vinyl wrong sides facing and sew around the outside.
- Neaten the edges with either a small zigzag stitch or encase with bias binding.
- Decorate the placemat as you wish with different coloured vinyls, ribbons,
  zigzag tape and bias binding.

Festive Gift Sack

Special occasions and festive holidays need not exclude your pets. Hang up a cheerful fish-shaped gift sack for your cat and fill it with an assortment of irresistible treats. If you decorate your home on such occasions, remember that shiny toy decorations are attractive to cats so be sure that they are not too small and can't be swallowed in play.

You will need

Template A
  (Page 57 – for backing)
Template B
  (Page 57 – for pocket)
1/2 m felt or fabric
1/2 m iron-on stiffener
Materials to decorate
10 cm ribbon or cord

To make

- Enlarge template A by 200% on a photocopier and use it to cut out two pieces of felt.
- Cut one piece of stiffener using template A.

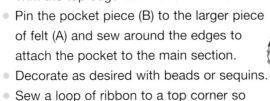

- Iron the stiffener onto one side of one piece of felt.
- Pin the two pieces of felt together, with the stiffener facing inwards and neatly sew around the edges to make one piece.
- Enlarge template B by 200% on a photocopier and use it to cut out one piece of felt for the pocket.
- Trim the top edge with ribbon and decorate further as you wish.
- Pin the pocket piece (B) to the larger piece of felt (A) and sew around the edges to attach the pocket to the main section.
- Decorate as desired with beads or sequins.
- Sew a loop of ribbon to a top corner so that the sack can be hung up.

GIFT IDEAS

Potato Prints

Potato printing is fun and easy to do. It is a wonderful way to personalise fabrics and any number of materials to be used for making toys, beds and fun items for your cats and friends.

You will need

Large potato

Pencil

Sharp craft knife or vegetable knife

Shallow dish to hold the paint

Fabric paint

Cotton fabric suitable for printing, e.g. calico

To make

- Decide on your design – simpler designs produce the best results.
- Cut the potato in half.
- Using the pencil, draw your design (or trace from a template if easier) onto the inside of each potato half.
- Carefully cut away around the *outside* of the design, so the pattern is raised on one half of the potato, and then cut away the *inside* of the design on the other half, so the pattern is recessed.
- Cover the bottom of the dish with paint.
- Dip the potato half with the recessed design into the dish and print onto the fabric. Repeat with the raised design.
- You can wash the potato and change the colour of the print at any time.
- Once the paint has dried, iron the fabric to set the paint.

Feline Frames

Photo frames are always a well-received gift. Most cat lovers would value a personalised frame to show off a picture of their beloved feline friend.

You will need

A4 piece of thick cardboard
Fake fur fabric off-cuts
Strong, quick-drying glue

To make

- Cut out a photo frame from the thick card, making sure that the inner dimension is slightly smaller than your photograph (see diagram 1).
- Glue the frame onto the back of a piece of fabric that has been cut to a size slightly larger than the frame (see diagram 2).
- Cut out the fabric inside the frame leaving a 2 cm edge to glue over the edges. Make a small cut in each corner of the fabric, both inside and outside the frame, and glue the edges down onto the back of the frame (see diagram 3).
- Let the glue dry. Insert your photograph and seal up the back of the frame.
- You can also use old photo frames that need some brightening up.

Diagram 1

Diagram 2

Diagram 3

Diagram 4

It is fun to take imprints of your tiny kitten's paws when he first arrives, and then as he grows to track his progress.

Purrfect Pawprints

Plaster of Paris pawprints are fun and easy to make. They can be painted and used to decorate items such as picture frames or feeding bowls, or simply be mounted on their own.

You will need
A shallow dish
Enough damp, fine sand to fill
   the dish halfway
A willing cat
A small bag of Plaster of Paris
Craft knife

To make
- Fill the dish with the damp sand and compact it firmly.
- Gently push your cat's paw down into the sand.
- Mix the Plaster of Paris into a runny paste that pours easily.
- Pour the mixture over the back of a spoon and into the imprint in the sand.
- Leave the Plaster of Paris to dry overnight.
- Gently turn the dish over and remove the imprint of the cat's paw. Brush off any remaining sand and use the craft knife to tidy the edges of the mould.

Caring for Orphaned Kittens

A kitten may need hand-raising because its mother has died, become ill, rejected the kitten or abandoned it. Raising an orphaned kitten is a noble and rewarding experience. The bonding that occurs in the first few days is likely to last a lifetime. However, orphaned kittens are very fragile and raising them requires a great deal of dedication and time; it is not a task to be taken on lightly.

Kittens should not be taken from their mother before eight weeks of age if possible. The longer the mother cat is able to feed the kittens, the better, since they need their mother's milk for nutrition as well as for important antibodies that protect them from disease. Kittens receive antibodies from their mothers in the form of colostrum within the first 24 to 48 hours of birth, and will almost certainly die if they do not receive this nourishing substance. Kittens also learn important behavioural lessons from their mothers, including hunting techniques and play/prey skills.

If you find or are given an orphaned kitten, first try finding a foster feline mother; breeders, your local vet and animal shelters may know of nursing cats in your area. Try calling any 'cat people' that you know for leads as well. Nursing mother cats will very often feed kittens other than their own.

If you must feed the kitten yourself before weaning age, you will have to devote considerable energy and weeks of constant care if the kitten is to have a good chance at survival. The younger the kitten, the more fragile it is. Very young kittens may not survive without a mother no matter how good the care.

Warmth and first aid

As soon as you find an orphaned kitten it must be protected from becoming chilled. Place it under your clothes next to your skin. Normally the mother cat and littermates would provide warmth. Kittens cannot regulate their own body temperature until four to five weeks of age and need to be kept in a box with sufficient blankets for them to burrow in if cold, and with high enough sides to keep out draughts. During their first week, they should be kept at temperatures of between 31 and 33 °C. For the next two weeks they need temperatures of approximately 27 °C. When they reach approximately five weeks they can tolerate a lower room temperature.

If possible, take the kitten to a veterinarian to be examined for dehydration and general condition. They can become dehydrated very quickly without a mother and may need fluids intravenously. Kittens that become dehydrated from a lack of fluids or diarrhoea will have very little energy or appetite and it is important to take care of this immediately.

Your vet will be able to offer advice and tips on hand-raising kittens as well as the necessary supplies you will need. Your vet will also be able to weigh the kitten on arrival, after which you can weigh it once a week to determine weight gain. They should almost double their weight weekly in the first few weeks, and then gain weight more slowly thereafter.

Feeding an orphaned kitten

As with any baby, all utensils should be sterilized carefully before each feeding. Total nutrition for newborn orphans must be supplied by a milk replacer which you can purchase from good pet stores or your local vet. The kitten will be fed with this until it is about three weeks old, after which you can introduce it to solid food. A commercial kitten milk replacer is the best thing to feed orphaned kitten. However, for short-term emergencies you can use the following ingredients in a uniformly blended mixture:

1 cup full-cream milk (not long-life)
1 or 2 tablespoons fresh cream
   (depending on whether the
   kitten is severely malnourished
   or reasonably healthy)
1 teaspoon glucose powder
   (obtainable from your chemist)
1 teaspoon Vidalin M or other
   paediatric vitamin and
   mineral supplement
1 egg yolk (no white)

● Decant for each feed and warm to body temperature.

Commercial milk replacers have directions on their labels for proper amounts to feed. Make sure you weigh the kitten accurately to avoid over- or underfeeding. A four-week-old kitten should receive 20 to 25% of its body weight in milk in a 24 hour period, i.e. a 200 g kitten should receive a total of 40 to 50 ml of milk divided into 6 to 8 feeds per day.

The milk replacer should be warmed to 35 to 38 °C for best results. Testing the milk replacer's temperature on your forearm, as for human babies, is generally accurate enough. The milk replacer should be about the same temperature as your skin, or slightly warmer. As the kitten grows older, the milk replacer can be fed at room temperature and does not need to be warmed up.

Dropper or syringe feeding is one of the best ways to feed very young kittens, spoonfeeding is very difficult and can result in food entering the kitten's lungs, which can cause drowning. Spoonfeeding is therefore not recommended. Baby bottles made for kittens can also be used quite successfully in most situations. The size of the hole in the nipple is critical for success. If the bottle is turned upside down and milk replacer drips from the nipple, the hole is too large. Use of this nipple may cause the kitten to drown. If the bottle is turned upside down and milk replacer comes out only after considerable squeezing of the bottle, the hole is too small. Use of this nipple will result in the kitten becoming discouraged and refusing to nurse. The hole is the proper size if the bottle is turned upside down and milk replacer drips from the nipple with minimal squeezing of the bottle.

To feed the kitten, place it on its stomach on a towel. Open its mouth gently and then slip the nipple, syringe or dropper between its jaws. Hold the bottle at a 45° angle. Feed approximately 5 to 10 ml at a time, depending on how much is being given at each feed.

Weaning

You may begin weaning the kitten at three weeks of age. Kittens cannot lap at less than four weeks of age and will choke if they try to. Start with a thick 'pap' of kitten food and formula mixed and warmed, offered on the finger until the kitten sucks it off. Milk feeds should remain the same until it is clear that a substantial amount of 'pap' is being eaten at each feed (starting with one or two a day, increasing to three of four 'pap' feeds a day and decreasing the milk feeds accordingly). Hand feeding can generally be stopped by the fourth week. By this time the kitten should be able to eat from a dish.

By four to four and a half weeks, the orphaned kitten should be able to consume enough moistened solid food to meet its needs. Don't expect the kitten to be weaned overnight. Also remember that changes in diet or certain foods can cause diarrhoea, so keep an eye out for this. Diarrhoea can be life threatening to a young kitten.

Toilet training

A kitten's natural mother licks the kitten's abdomen to stimulate the bowels and bladder, and tidies up the resulting mess. As the surrogate mother, gently rub the kitten's abdomen and bottom with a cotton ball or pad moistened with warm water to accomplish this. This will stimulate the discharge of waste and keep the kitten clean. Be careful to rub gently and only enough to expel waste materials. If this procedure is not followed, the kitten may become constipated. Keep the area clean and watch for chafing, which might indicate that you are rubbing too hard or not cleaning well enough. Vaseline can be used around the anus if it becomes red or inflamed. If the kitten has diarrhoea and becomes caked with stool, wash it in warm water as this is gentle on their skin. If you need to clean the kitten, wash its fur all over with a damp face cloth using short strokes as the mother cat would.

The four-week mark is a good time to introduce the kitten to the litter box. Place the kitten in the box after each meal. You may have to take the kitten's paw and show it how to scratch in the litter – they usually catch on quickly.

Fleas and parasites

Abandoned kittens will need to be checked for and cleared of fleas and parasites as soon as possible. Your vet will have flea sprays and dewormers that are suitable for use on kittens. Always check the manufacturer's instructions before use.

Milestones

* At birth, a kitten should weigh 60 to 120 grams.
* By the end of its first week it should double its body weight.
* The kitten should open its eyes at about eight days.
* The eyes will stay blue for about two weeks after opening. The true eye colour will not appear until the kitten is about three months old.
* At two weeks the ears will start to stand up.
* At about three weeks the kitten will try to walk.
* At four weeks kittens start to play with each other and develop teeth.

Grooming in cats is necessary to stimulate new hair growth, to remove loose hair, to prevent matting of the coat, and to spread secretions from glands on the skin so that the coat is kept waterproof and their bodies remain insulated. Cats start learning to groom themselves using their barbed tongues as combs when they are about three weeks old. This behaviour is instinctive and they can usually groom themselves with ease at six weeks.

Most shorthaired cats are exceptionally proficient at self-grooming and need very little, if any, help to keep their coats in tip-top condition. However, this does not mean we can't join in and use the grooming time not only as a time for bonding with our cats, but also as a time when we can check their physical well-being.

Cats often enjoy being groomed by their owners. Once they get used to having their coats combed and brushed, grooming becomes an enjoyable experience for both cat and owner. It is a good idea to get your cat used to being groomed when he is still a kitten so he will become accustomed to the experience. Long-haired cats will need to be groomed every day, while the shorter-haired types will need brushing less frequently. It is wise, however, to establish a weekly routine in order for you to become familiar with your cat's body so any changes or abnormalities can be recognised and caught at an early stage.

Tools required

Brushes: The type of brush depends on the breed of cat you have, but a soft bristle brush is usually suitable.

Comb: A metal-toothed comb is ideal for removing dead hair; make sure that the teeth have rounded edges so that they will not scratch the cat.

Grooming glove: A grooming glove is used to put a shine on your cat's coat, you can use a piece of silk cloth for the short-haired varieties.

Cotton balls: Used for wiping ears and eyes.

Nail clippers: Guillotine clippers are the safest choice.

Animal toothpaste: Never use human toothpaste as it foams and cats dislike this intensely.

A baby's toothbrush

- Start your grooming routine by stroking your cat in order to relax him and put him at ease. Part the hair to check the roots for flea dirt, ticks and any skin irritations. Run your hands over his body to check for scars or wounds. Check ears for wounds, mites or encrustations. Check eyes and nose for discharges. Check the cat's teeth, looking for any tartar, gingivitis, mouth ulcers or sore gums. Check his claws for ragged edges or cuts. Examine under your cat's tail for sore spots and worm segments.

- Place the cat on a clean, white surface for brushing so you can examine the brushings for flea dirt. Brushing should be an enjoyable experience for your cat. Hold him gently but firmly and start by brushing him along his back, then brush his legs, head, belly and finish at his tail. Loose hair that is not removed by brushing may be swallowed by the cat when he cleans himself, causing a blockage in the stomach known as a fur ball. Stop at any time if you notice that the cat is becoming agitated or afraid. Short-haired cats will need to be brushed only, but you may find you will need to comb the longer haired varieties as well to remove knots and tangles.
- Using the metal comb, comb through the hair in the direction that it grows. Be careful not pull on the hair. Ensure the whole body is combed, paying special attention under the elbows, between the hind legs and along the sides of the tail.

- Cleaning the ears should rarely be necessary. If the ears have scabs or encrustations, the cat may have an infection – this will need to be looked at by your vet. Never poke anything into the ear. The inside of the earflap can be wiped gently with a damp cotton ball if necessary.

- Use a moistened cotton wool ball to clean the eyes if necessary. The ball can be moistened with a weak saline solution or a commercially available tearstain remover. This can be found at most pet shops or from your vet; it is used mainly by breeders who show their cats.

- Tooth decay and gum disease in domestic cats is usually a sign of a bad diet, most vets in small practice agree that over 95% of cats they examine have tooth decay. If you are going to clean your cat's teeth, make sure you start when the cat is very young so it will become accustomed to the experience. Special cat and animal toothpaste is available; this is best used on a finger brush or a small baby's toothbrush so you can carefully control the brushing.

- The vast majority of cats will not need to have their nails clipped. However, if you have an indoor cat and need to clip its nails, you will need patience and practice. Hold the cat's paw still and gently extend the claws so that the tips are clearly visible. Clip off a very small amount of nail from the tip. It is better to remove a small amount initially and remove more later if necessary rather than causing injury or pain by taking off too much at first.

- To finish, use the grooming glove to put a really healthy shine on your cat's coat. Simply stroke the cat in the direction of hair growth to polish the hair.